THE BEST BOOK OF

Knights and Castles

Deborah Murrell

KINGFISHER

BOSTON

Contents

KINGFISHER

a Houghton Mifflin Company imprint
222 Berkeley Street
Boston, Massachusetts 02116
www.houghtonmifflinbooks.com

Author: Deborah Murrell
Consultant: Professor Norman Housley
Editorial director: Melissa Fairley
Coordinating editor: Caitlin Doyle
Art director: Mike Davis
DTP coordinator: Susanne Olbrich
DTP operator: Primrose Burton
Senior production controller: Lindsey Scott
Artwork archivist: Wendy Allison
Proofreader: Sheila Clewley
Indexer: Rebecca Fairley

*Main illustrations by Chris Molan
and Mark Bergin*

First published in 2005

10 9 8 7 6 5 4 3 2 1
1TR/0605/WKT/SOLGRA(SOLGRA)/128KMA/C

Copyright © Kingfisher
Publications Plc 2005

LIBRARY OF CONGRESS CATALOGING-IN-PUBLICATION DATA
Murrell, Deborah Jane, 1963–
The best book of knights and castles/
Deborah Murrell.—1st ed.
    p. cm.
Includes index.
1. Knights and knighthood—Juvenile literature. 2.
Castles—Juvenile literature. 3. Civilization,
Medieval—Juvenile literature. I. Title.
CR4513.M87 2005
940.1—dc22   2005006224

ISBN 0-7534-5935-3
ISBN 978-07534-5935-5

Printed in China

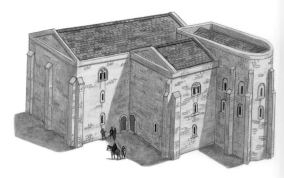

 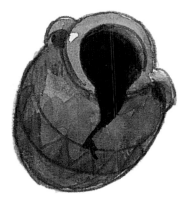 

The Norman invasion

When King Edward of England died in 1066, Harold was crowned king. William of Normandy—a region in northern France—thought that he should be the king and invaded England. He defeated Harold in the Battle of Hastings and seized the throne. William, now called William the Conqueror, built many castles to subdue the English people.

Castle building

The first castles were simple and made out of wood. They often consisted of a mound of earth (a motte) next to a courtyard (a bailey). The height of the motte made it easy to see enemies approaching, so the owner often built a watchtower on it. Soldiers could look out for danger through holes in the tower walls.

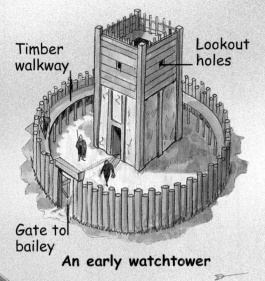

Timber walkway

Lookout holes

Gate to bailey

An early watchtower

A Norman motte and bailey

People and animals lived in the bailey. It was surrounded by a ditch and a fence, often with a bridge that could be lifted up in order to help keep enemies out. If the bailey was attacked, the people retreated to the motte. Some larger castles had a great hall on top of the motte, where the lord and his family lived.

Stone castles

Wooden castles were quick to build, but they could burn down easily. Lords who could afford it began to build castles out of stone. A medieval king's or rich lord's castle would also have been used as a garrison—a home for the knights who protected him.

Master builders

Men who could design stone buildings were highly paid and well respected. One of the best known was named Gundulf. He traveled to England from Normandy soon after William the Conqueror became king. Gundulf designed the cathedral and castle in Rochester, England, where he was the bishop, as well as the White Tower at the Tower of London, England.

Fighting on the stairs

The spiral staircase was usually built with the central pillar on the left (if you were coming down the stairs). This meant that defending soldiers, who would be fighting as they moved down the stairs, had their right arms free to wield (swing) their swords. The attackers would be trying to climb the stairs, and their right arms would have less space.

Ivry-la-Bataille

This castle was built in Normandy, France, in the A.D. 900s or 1000s. It may have inspired castle builders in England to build similar tall stone towers.

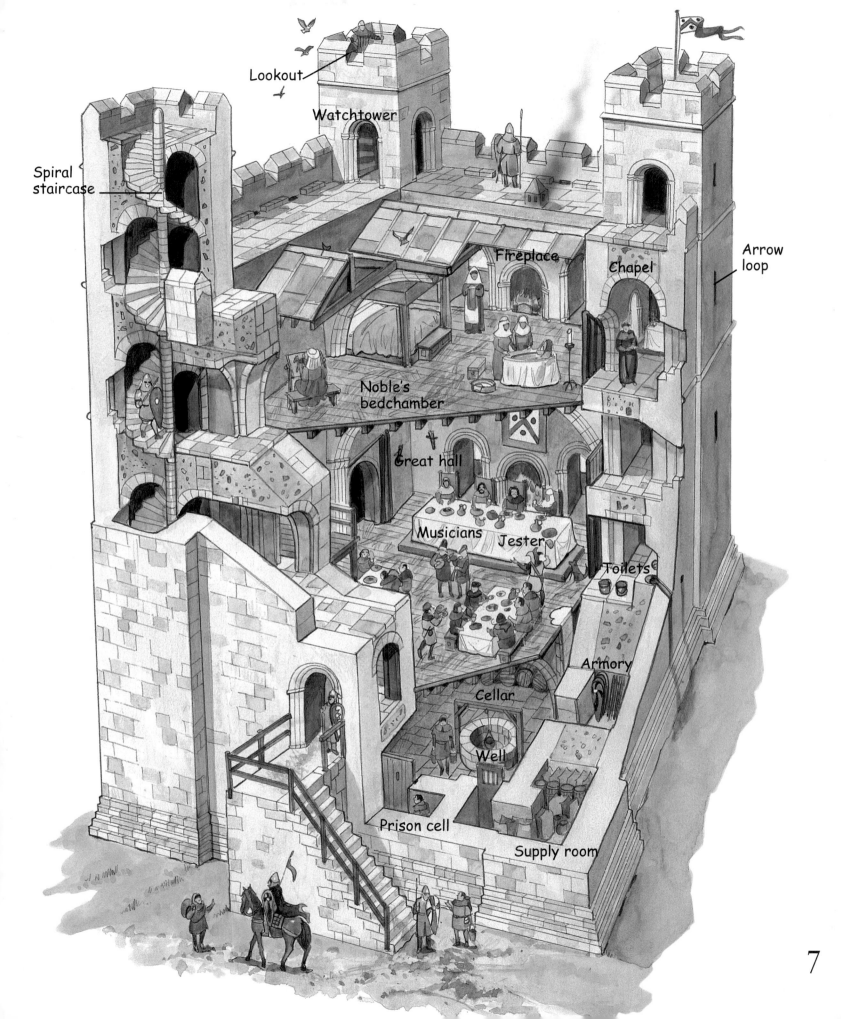

Lookout

Spiral
staircase

Watchtower

Fireplace

Chapel

Arrow
loop

Noble's
bedchamber

Great hall

Musicians

Jester

Toilets

Armory

Cellar

Well

Prison cell

Supply room

7

Medieval life

Medieval kings divided their land between the nobles, who were usually also knights. In exchange, the nobles promised to fight for the king when it was necessary and to supply other knights for fighting. These knights often lived in the noble's manor house and helped protect it. Most of them came from wealthy families, since training and arming a knight was an expensive task.

Describing a knight

The word for "knight" was different in each country. In Spain they were called *caballeros* and in France, *chevalier*. Both meant a warrior who fought on horseback.

Kneeling knight

Knights were expected to behave politely and humbly to noblewomen. This knight is kneeling to receive a "favor" (scarf) from the lady.

A knight might carry a favor at a tournament.

Men, women, and children all worked in the fields at harvesttime.

In addition to nobles, the king also gave land to the bishops and abbots. Many of them were as powerful as the nobles. Religious men and women were often the most educated people in society.

A reeve, or overseer, might be in charge of other peasants.

In exchange for farming the lord's land, peasants were allowed to farm a small area of land in order to feed themselves and their families.

9

Becoming a knight

There were three stages in becoming a knight. From around the age of seven boys would be sent to the home of a lord. They were called pages, and they served the lord and lady and learned basic social etiquette and fighting skills. From the age of 14 pages who had succeeded in the basic training became squires. They learned more advanced fighting skills and acted as a knight's assistant. A squire would hope to be knighted by the time he was 21 years old.

A page's lessons

Pages had to learn how to fight with swords and other weapons. For safety they practiced with weapons made out of wood. Pages also had to learn Latin. They were usually taught by the chaplain.

Before being allowed to ride a real horse, a page had his first riding lessons on a wooden horse. This was safer and also avoided the risk of expensive horses being injured during training.

From squire to knight
Only the king or another knight could make a squire a knight. This was called "dubbing" and was done by tapping the squire on the shoulders and head with a sword.

Squire

11

Armor and weapons

During the Middle Ages many advances were made in the armor and weapons used by knights. Early armor was made out of chain mail, which protected a knight against slashing blows. Later plate armor became available. This was more protective, but it was also more expensive. Only very wealthy knights could afford armor for their horses as well.

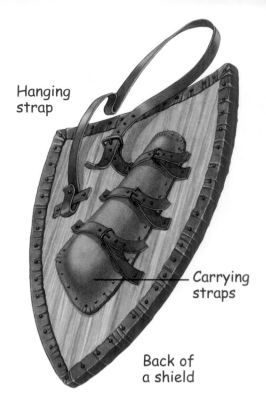

Hanging strap

Carrying straps

Back of a shield

Shields were made out of wood. Early shields were almost as big as the knights themselves. As time went by and armor became more effective, shields became smaller.

Extra padding

Chain mail was made up of thousands of tiny iron rings. Knights wore a padded undershirt, which helped protect them against heavy blows. It also helped stop the chain mail from scratching their skin and making them uncomfortable.

Rust was removed from chain mail by rolling it in sand.

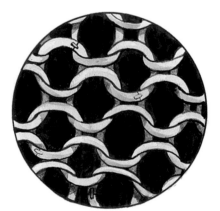

Chain mail was made from many interlocking rings.

12

Armor plating

Plate armor was made out of sheets of metal. The knight's knees, elbows, and other joints were covered with many overlapping pieces. These were loosely joined together so that the knight could move his arms and legs.

Chain mail and plate armor weighed around the same amount. Plate armor felt lighter to the person wearing it, since the weight rested more evenly on the body.

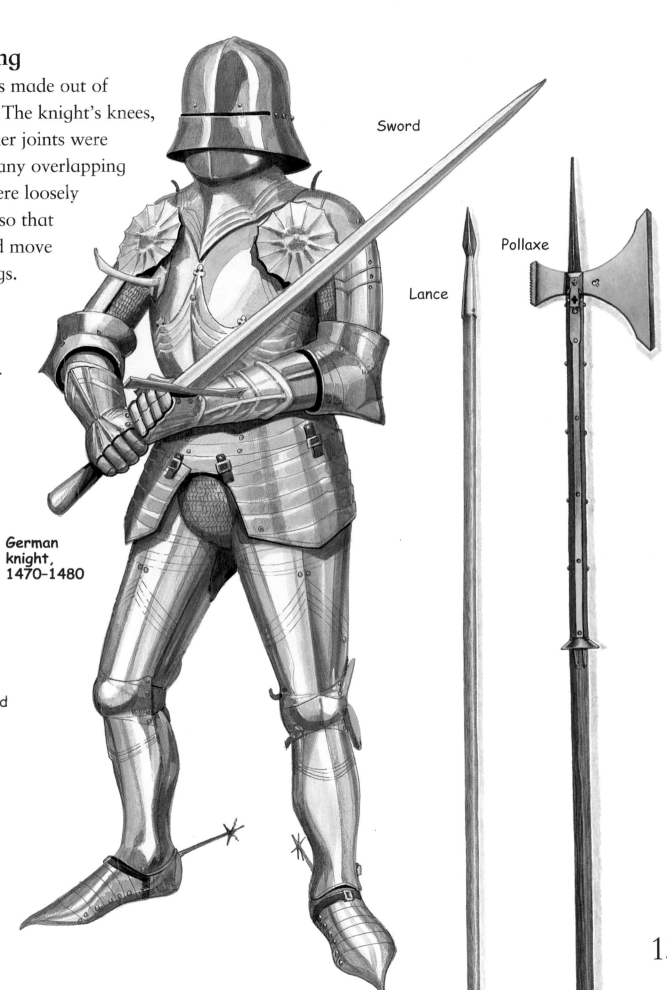

Sword

Lance

Pollaxe

German knight, 1470–1480

Flailed mace

13

Heraldry

When knights wore armor and helmets, it was difficult to tell them apart. They started wearing symbols on their tunics, shields, and helmets so that other knights could recognize them. These symbols developed into coats of arms. Families, towns—and even some companies—still have coats of arms today.

A city crest

This coat of arms belongs to the city of Lancaster, England. The words read "Luck to Loyne," which is the river from which the city took its name.

Helms and crests

In tournaments knights often wore a great helm. This type of helmet covered the entire head, with slits to see through and holes for breathing. A helm hid the face, so many knights added a crest so that people would know who they were.

Mythical creatures

Many crests and coats of arms showed mythical creatures. The unicorn is a symbol of purity and virtue.

Tree of chivalry

A real or artificial tree of chivalry was often used at a tournament. Heralds hung their knights' shields on the tree to show who was taking part in the competition.

Tournaments

When they were not at war, knights practiced their skills by fighting each other in tournaments. There could be several events in a tournament, including jousting. Early jousts were violent and dangerous, so people invented rules in order to make them safer.

Jousting

In a joust two knights rode toward each other, aiming their lances at the other knight's shield. They won points if they hit the shield and lost points if they broke the tip of their lance on the other knight's lance.

Swan crest ———————— on the helm

Specially shaped shield to steady the lance

A knight who knocked another knight off his horse won full points.

Fighting before a battle

When they were away from home, knights got bored. For entertainment they often organized tournaments between opposing armies. The leaders of the armies tried to stop these events, because knights could die before the next battle.

Riding skills

In "running the rings" knights took turns galloping their horses past a post. They had to try and hook small hoops off the post and onto their lances. This was a good test of accuracy and riding skills.

Barrier separating the knights

Holy wars

Jerusalem, in Israel, was a holy place for Muslims, Christians, and Jews. It was ruled by Muslim people, who allowed Christians to travel there safely. Then Muslim Seljuks took control, and it became dangerous for Christians to go to the Holy Land. The pope called for Christians to lead a crusade (holy war) against the Seljuks. This began hundreds of years of fighting in the Middle East and Europe.

Richard I

The King of England, Richard I (1157–1199), won great fame for his fighting against the Saracens—the name the Christians gave to Saladin's army.

Saladin

In 1099 the Christians captured Jerusalem. The Christians ruled the Holy Land for almost 100 years. In 1187 Saladin, the ruler of Egypt, united the Muslims and recaptured it. Saladin was one of the most civilized rulers in the world at the time. When Richard I had a fever, Saladin sent him snow to cool him down.

Both Saracens and Christian knights fought on horseback.

A crusader castle

When the Christians captured the Holy Land, they tried to strengthen its defenses. They needed castles to use as army bases, as well as to guard roads and borders. Krak des Chevaliers was a small Muslim fortress. The Christian Knights Hospitallers rebuilt it, adding two solid outer walls.

Lookout tower

Commander's room

Aqueduct

Water reservoir

A winning trick

The Christian Knights Hospitallers controlled Krak des Chevaliers from 1124 to 1271, when a group of Muslims called Baybars attacked it. The leader of the Baybars tricked the defending knights with a fake letter from their Grand Master, telling them to surrender.

Inner courtyard

Main hall

Covered walkway

Fighting base

Krak des Chevaliers could house up to 2,000 knights and store enough food to feed a large army for one year. The castle survived at least 12 attacks before it fell to the Baybars.

Military orders

Some of the knights who stayed in the Holy Land formed military orders. They lived religious lives, like monks, but they were also highly respected warriors who fought for their religion. In the Third Crusade the Knights Templar and Hospitallers marched at the front and back of Richard I's army to protect the troops.

Protecting pilgrims

The Knights Templar (below) promised to protect pilgrims (religious visitors to the Holy Land). Instead of the wool robes that most monks wore, they were allowed to wear linen, because of the heat in the Middle East.

Going east

In their early days Teutonic knights ran a hospital. They became more militant in the late 1100s and traveled to eastern Europe to convert the Slav people to Christianity.

Healing and trading

The Knights Hospitallers took care of the sick. They owned a fleet of ships, which they used to trade goods, such as spices and silks, between the Middle East and Europe.

Siege warfare

Castles had such strong defenses that sometimes the only way to capture one was to besiege it by surrounding it with troops. People built special machines, called siege engines, to attack a castle and persuade the soldiers defending it to surrender.

Slings and arrows

Some machines, such as the trebuchet and the ballista, slung stones and other objects over the walls of a castle. Belfries, or siege towers, carried troops right up to the castle, where they could fight the soldiers on top. Sappers, or miners, tried to dig beneath the walls.

Trebuchet

Château Gaillard, France, under siege in 1204

Belfry

Sappers

Catapult

Battering ram

25

The end of an era

 By the late Middle Ages the time of the warrior knight was coming to an end. There were many reasons for this. Money, advances in weapons and warfare, and international politics all played a role in the disappearance of the medieval knight. Today some countries still dub knights, but it is simply a symbol of respect, and knights are not expected to fight for their country.

Ruined castles

Many knights returned home to manage their estates (lands). Castles were not strong enough to stand up to cannons, so those who could afford to built stronger fortresses. Some castles remained, but many fell into ruins, and their stones were used for new buildings.

Shooting power

Guns and gunpowder were invented in the 1300s, and by the 1400s they were often used in wars. Even plate armor could not protect a knight or his horse from bullets. Many military leaders began to hire professional, full-time soldiers, who were always available for fighting and training, instead of relying on knights to fight when they were needed.

Castles today

Some medieval castles still stand today. Many are open to visitors and contain museum collections or other exhibitions. Over hundreds of years people have added towers and rebuilt parts of castles. Some castles today look very different than the way that they were originally designed.

The Tower of London

Since it was built, the Tower of London, in England, has been used at different times as a prison, a supply room, and a museum. The White Tower—completed around 1097—was the first stone keep in England. It is one of the most popular tourist attractions in Great Britain.

Beefeaters, the Tower of London's guards, give daily tours for visitors.

Saumur Castle

Saumur Castle, in France, was built in the 1300s. Today it is open to visitors and contains a museum with a collection of medieval art.

How do we know?

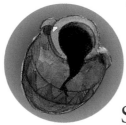

We **can** discover more about knights, castles, and medieval life from a wide range of things.

Some castles and their contents, such as furniture and common household objects, have survived. These items can tell us what life in a castle was like. Stories and letters tell us what people found interesting. Even gravestones can tell us what type of clothing and armor people wore.

Hidden history

Sometimes medieval floors lie underneath more recent ones. Archaeologists uncovering them are very careful not to damage them.

Glossary

aqueduct A man-made channel created to move water from a river or lake to a town or building.

archer A soldier who fought with a bow and arrows.

armory A place where arms, or weapons, were stored.

arrow loop A slit in the side of a castle or other building, used for firing arrows through.

battering ram A heavy object—often a wooden beam—that attackers swung or rammed against a door to break it down.

cannon A large, heavy gun used in warfare to fire cannonballs.

catapult A machine used to throw large rocks or other heavy objects.

chaplain A religious man who worked outside of the church.

favor An object, such as a handkerchief, that a noblewoman gave to a knight to wear in order to show his loyalty to her.

garrison A group of soldiers who defended a castle, fortress, or town, as well as the building or part of the building in which they lived.

great hall A castle's main area, where people ate, had meetings, and slept.

jester A joker, paid by a noble family to entertain them.

mace A heavy club with a solid metal end, sometimes spiked.

medieval Relates to the Middle Ages.

Middle Ages A period of history in Europe, often said to be from around A.D. 1000–1500.

pollaxe A long weapon with a hammer or spiked axe at the end.

siege tower A tall tower with a stairway that could be wheeled up to a castle, also known as a belfry. Soldiers climbed up it to enter the castle over the walls.

trebuchet A type of catapult with a long, weighted arm, used to throw objects over castle walls.

Index